CONFIDENTIAL
CONFIDENTIAL
CONFIDENTIAL
CONFIDENTIAL

Character Index

Character Name	Story/World	Page #

Character Index

Character Name	Story/World	Page #

CHARACTER NAME :

NICKNAME/ALIAS:

AGE:

DATE OF BIRTH:

WHERE ARE THEY FROM?:

CURRENT LOCATION:

EDUCATION:

PHYSICAL DESCRIPTION:

FAMILY HISTORY:

SOCIAL BACKGROUND:

RELIGION:

HOBBIES:

POSITIVE CHARACTERISTICS:

NEGATIVE CHARACTERISTICS:

GOALS:

LIKES: DISLIKES:

FRIENDS: ENEMIES:

CHARACTER ARC/DEVELOPMENT:

ADDITIONAL CHARACTER DETAILS FOR:

CHARACTER NAME :

NICKNAME/ALIAS:

AGE:

DATE OF BIRTH:

WHERE ARE THEY FROM?:

CURRENT LOCATION:

EDUCATION:

PHYSICAL DESCRIPTION:

FAMILY HISTORY:

SOCIAL BACKGROUND:

RELIGION:

HOBBIES:

POSITIVE CHARACTERISTICS:

NEGATIVE CHARACTERISTICS:

GOALS:

LIKES: DISLIKES:

FRIENDS: ENEMIES:

CHARACTER ARC/DEVELOPMENT:

ADDITIONAL CHARACTER DETAILS FOR:

CHARACTER NAME :

NICKNAME/ALIAS:

AGE:

DATE OF BIRTH:

WHERE ARE THEY FROM?:

CURRENT LOCATION:

EDUCATION:

PHYSICAL DESCRIPTION:

FAMILY HISTORY:

SOCIAL BACKGROUND:

RELIGION:

HOBBIES:

POSITIVE CHARACTERISTICS:

NEGATIVE CHARACTERISTICS:

GOALS:

LIKES: DISLIKES:

FRIENDS: ENEMIES:

CHARACTER ARC/DEVELOPMENT:

ADDITIONAL CHARACTER DETAILS FOR:

CHARACTER NAME :

NICKNAME/ALIAS:

AGE:

DATE OF BIRTH:

WHERE ARE THEY FROM?:

CURRENT LOCATION:

EDUCATION:

PHYSICAL DESCRIPTION:

FAMILY HISTORY:

SOCIAL BACKGROUND:

RELIGION:

HOBBIES:

POSITIVE CHARACTERISTICS:

NEGATIVE CHARACTERISTICS:

GOALS:

LIKES: DISLIKES:

FRIENDS: ENEMIES:

CHARACTER ARC/DEVELOPMENT:

ADDITIONAL CHARACTER DETAILS FOR:

CHARACTER NAME :

NICKNAME/ALIAS:

AGE:

DATE OF BIRTH:

WHERE ARE THEY FROM?:

CURRENT LOCATION:

EDUCATION:

PHYSICAL DESCRIPTION:

FAMILY HISTORY:

SOCIAL BACKGROUND:

RELIGION:

HOBBIES:

POSITIVE CHARACTERISTICS:

NEGATIVE CHARACTERISTICS:

GOALS:

LIKES: DISLIKES:

FRIENDS: ENEMIES:

CHARACTER ARC/DEVELOPMENT:

ADDITIONAL CHARACTER DETAILS FOR:

CHARACTER NAME :

NICKNAME/ALIAS:

AGE:

DATE OF BIRTH:

WHERE ARE THEY FROM?:

CURRENT LOCATION:

EDUCATION:

PHYSICAL DESCRIPTION:

FAMILY HISTORY:

SOCIAL BACKGROUND:

RELIGION:

HOBBIES:

POSITIVE CHARACTERISTICS:

NEGATIVE CHARACTERISTICS:

GOALS:

LIKES: DISLIKES:

FRIENDS: ENEMIES:

CHARACTER ARC/DEVELOPMENT:

ADDITIONAL CHARACTER DETAILS FOR:

CHARACTER NAME :

NICKNAME/ALIAS:

AGE:

DATE OF BIRTH:

WHERE ARE THEY FROM?:

CURRENT LOCATION:

EDUCATION:

PHYSICAL DESCRIPTION:

FAMILY HISTORY:

SOCIAL BACKGROUND:

RELIGION:

HOBBIES:

POSITIVE CHARACTERISTICS:

NEGATIVE CHARACTERISTICS:

GOALS:

LIKES: DISLIKES:

FRIENDS: ENEMIES:

DEVELOPMENT:

CHARACTER NAME :

NICKNAME/ALIAS:

AGE:

DATE OF BIRTH:

WHERE ARE THEY FROM?:

CURRENT LOCATION:

EDUCATION:

PHYSICAL DESCRIPTION:

FAMILY HISTORY:

SOCIAL BACKGROUND:

RELIGION:

HOBBIES:

POSITIVE CHARACTERISTICS:

NEGATIVE CHARACTERISTICS:

GOALS:

LIKES: DISLIKES:

FRIENDS: ENEMIES:

CHARACTER ARC/DEVELOPMENT:

ADDITIONAL CHARACTER DETAILS FOR:

CHARACTER NAME :

NICKNAME/ALIAS:

AGE:

DATE OF BIRTH:

WHERE ARE THEY FROM?:

CURRENT LOCATION:

EDUCATION:

PHYSICAL DESCRIPTION:

FAMILY HISTORY:

SOCIAL BACKGROUND:

RELIGION:

HOBBIES:

POSITIVE CHARACTERISTICS:

NEGATIVE CHARACTERISTICS:

GOALS:

LIKES: DISLIKES:

FRIENDS: ENEMIES:

CHARACTER ARC/DEVELOPMENT:

ADDITIONAL CHARACTER DETAILS FOR:

CHARACTER NAME :

NICKNAME/ALIAS:

AGE:

DATE OF BIRTH:

WHERE ARE THEY FROM?:

CURRENT LOCATION:

EDUCATION:

PHYSICAL DESCRIPTION:

FAMILY HISTORY:

SOCIAL BACKGROUND:

RELIGION:

HOBBIES:

POSITIVE CHARACTERISTICS:

NEGATIVE CHARACTERISTICS:

GOALS:

LIKES: DISLIKES:

FRIENDS: ENEMIES:

CHARACTER ARC/DEVELOPMENT:

ADDITIONAL CHARACTER DETAILS FOR:

CHARACTER NAME :

NICKNAME/ALIAS:

AGE:

DATE OF BIRTH:

WHERE ARE THEY FROM?:

CURRENT LOCATION:

EDUCATION:

PHYSICAL DESCRIPTION:

FAMILY HISTORY:

SOCIAL BACKGROUND:

RELIGION:

HOBBIES:

POSITIVE CHARACTERISTICS:

NEGATIVE CHARACTERISTICS:

GOALS:

LIKES: DISLIKES:

FRIENDS: ENEMIES:

CHARACTER ARC/DEVELOPMENT:

ADDITIONAL CHARACTER DETAILS FOR:

CHARACTER NAME :

NICKNAME/ALIAS:

AGE:

DATE OF BIRTH:

WHERE ARE THEY FROM?:

CURRENT LOCATION:

EDUCATION:

PHYSICAL DESCRIPTION:

FAMILY HISTORY:

SOCIAL BACKGROUND:

RELIGION:

HOBBIES:

POSITIVE CHARACTERISTICS:

NEGATIVE CHARACTERISTICS:

GOALS:

LIKES: DISLIKES:

FRIENDS: ENEMIES:

CHARACTER ARC/DEVELOPMENT:

CHARACTER NAME :

NICKNAME/ALIAS:

AGE:

DATE OF BIRTH:

WHERE ARE THEY FROM?:

CURRENT LOCATION:

EDUCATION:

PHYSICAL DESCRIPTION:

FAMILY HISTORY:

SOCIAL BACKGROUND:

RELIGION:

HOBBIES:

POSITIVE CHARACTERISTICS:

NEGATIVE CHARACTERISTICS:

GOALS:

LIKES: DISLIKES:

FRIENDS: ENEMIES:

CHARACTER ARC/DEVELOPMENT:

ADDITIONAL CHARACTER DETAILS FOR:

CHARACTER NAME :

NICKNAME/ALIAS:

AGE:

DATE OF BIRTH:

WHERE ARE THEY FROM?:

CURRENT LOCATION:

EDUCATION:

PHYSICAL DESCRIPTION:

FAMILY HISTORY:

SOCIAL BACKGROUND:

RELIGION:

HOBBIES:

POSITIVE CHARACTERISTICS:

NEGATIVE CHARACTERISTICS:

GOALS:

LIKES: DISLIKES:

FRIENDS: ENEMIES:

DEVELOPMENT:

ADDITIONAL CHARACTER DETAILS FOR:

CHARACTER NAME :

NICKNAME/ALIAS:

AGE:

DATE OF BIRTH:

WHERE ARE THEY FROM?:

CURRENT LOCATION:

EDUCATION:

PHYSICAL DESCRIPTION:

FAMILY HISTORY:

SOCIAL BACKGROUND:

RELIGION:

HOBBIES:

POSITIVE CHARACTERISTICS:

NEGATIVE CHARACTERISTICS:

GOALS:

LIKES: DISLIKES:

FRIENDS: ENEMIES:

CHARACTER ARC/DEVELOPMENT:

ADDITIONAL CHARACTER DETAILS FOR:

CHARACTER NAME :

NICKNAME/ALIAS:

AGE:

DATE OF BIRTH:

WHERE ARE THEY FROM?:

CURRENT LOCATION:

EDUCATION:

PHYSICAL DESCRIPTION:

FAMILY HISTORY:

SOCIAL BACKGROUND:

RELIGION:

HOBBIES:

POSITIVE CHARACTERISTICS:

NEGATIVE CHARACTERISTICS:

GOALS:

LIKES: DISLIKES:

FRIENDS: ENEMIES:

CHARACTER ARC/DEVELOPMENT:

ADDITIONAL CHARACTER DETAILS FOR:

CHARACTER NAME :

NICKNAME/ALIAS:

AGE:

DATE OF BIRTH:

WHERE ARE THEY FROM?:

CURRENT LOCATION:

EDUCATION:

PHYSICAL DESCRIPTION:

FAMILY HISTORY:

SOCIAL BACKGROUND:

RELIGION:

HOBBIES:

POSITIVE CHARACTERISTICS:

NEGATIVE CHARACTERISTICS:

GOALS:

LIKES: DISLIKES:

FRIENDS: ENEMIES:

CHARACTER ARC/DEVELOPMENT:

ADDITIONAL CHARACTER DETAILS FOR:

CHARACTER NAME :

NICKNAME/ALIAS:

AGE:

DATE OF BIRTH:

WHERE ARE THEY FROM?:

CURRENT LOCATION:

EDUCATION:

PHYSICAL DESCRIPTION:

FAMILY HISTORY:

SOCIAL BACKGROUND:

RELIGION:

HOBBIES:

POSITIVE CHARACTERISTICS:

NEGATIVE CHARACTERISTICS:

GOALS:

LIKES: DISLIKES:

FRIENDS: ENEMIES:

CHARACTER ARC/DEVELOPMENT:

ADDITIONAL CHARACTER DETAILS FOR:

CHARACTER NAME :

NICKNAME/ALIAS:

AGE:

DATE OF BIRTH:

WHERE ARE THEY FROM?:

CURRENT LOCATION:

EDUCATION:

PHYSICAL DESCRIPTION:

FAMILY HISTORY:

SOCIAL BACKGROUND:

RELIGION:

HOBBIES:

POSITIVE CHARACTERISTICS:

NEGATIVE CHARACTERISTICS:

GOALS:

LIKES: DISLIKES:

FRIENDS: ENEMIES:

CHARACTER ARC/DEVELOPMENT:

ADDITIONAL CHARACTER DETAILS FOR:

CHARACTER NAME :

NICKNAME/ALIAS:

AGE:

DATE OF BIRTH:

WHERE ARE THEY FROM?:

CURRENT LOCATION:

EDUCATION:

PHYSICAL DESCRIPTION:

FAMILY HISTORY:

SOCIAL BACKGROUND:

RELIGION:

HOBBIES:

POSITIVE CHARACTERISTICS:

NEGATIVE CHARACTERISTICS:

GOALS:

LIKES: DISLIKES:

FRIENDS: ENEMIES:

CHARACTER ARC/DEVELOPMENT:

ADDITIONAL CHARACTER DETAILS FOR:

CHARACTER NAME :

NICKNAME/ALIAS:

AGE:

DATE OF BIRTH:

WHERE ARE THEY FROM?:

CURRENT LOCATION:

EDUCATION:

PHYSICAL DESCRIPTION:

FAMILY HISTORY:

SOCIAL BACKGROUND:

RELIGION:

HOBBIES:

POSITIVE CHARACTERISTICS:

NEGATIVE CHARACTERISTICS:

GOALS:

LIKES: DISLIKES:

FRIENDS: ENEMIES:

DEVELOPMENT:

ADDITIONAL CHARACTER DETAILS FOR:

CHARACTER NAME :

NICKNAME/ALIAS:

AGE:

DATE OF BIRTH:

WHERE ARE THEY FROM?:

CURRENT LOCATION:

EDUCATION:

PHYSICAL DESCRIPTION:

FAMILY HISTORY:

SOCIAL BACKGROUND:

RELIGION:

HOBBIES:

POSITIVE CHARACTERISTICS:

NEGATIVE CHARACTERISTICS:

GOALS:

LIKES: DISLIKES:

FRIENDS: ENEMIES:

CHARACTER ARC/DEVELOPMENT:

ADDITIONAL CHARACTER DETAILS FOR:

CHARACTER NAME :

NICKNAME/ALIAS:

AGE:

DATE OF BIRTH:

WHERE ARE THEY FROM?:

CURRENT LOCATION:

EDUCATION:

PHYSICAL DESCRIPTION:

FAMILY HISTORY:

SOCIAL BACKGROUND:

RELIGION:

HOBBIES:

POSITIVE CHARACTERISTICS:

NEGATIVE CHARACTERISTICS:

GOALS:

LIKES: DISLIKES:

FRIENDS: ENEMIES:

CHARACTER ARC/DEVELOPMENT:

ADDITIONAL CHARACTER DETAILS FOR:

CHARACTER NAME :

NICKNAME/ALIAS:

AGE:

DATE OF BIRTH:

WHERE ARE THEY FROM?:

CURRENT LOCATION:

EDUCATION:

PHYSICAL DESCRIPTION:

FAMILY HISTORY:

SOCIAL BACKGROUND:

RELIGION:

HOBBIES:

POSITIVE CHARACTERISTICS:

NEGATIVE CHARACTERISTICS:

GOALS:

LIKES: DISLIKES:

FRIENDS: ENEMIES:

CHARACTER ARC/DEVELOPMENT:

ADDITIONAL CHARACTER DETAILS FOR:

CHARACTER NAME :

NICKNAME/ALIAS:

AGE:

DATE OF BIRTH:

WHERE ARE THEY FROM?:

CURRENT LOCATION:

EDUCATION:

PHYSICAL DESCRIPTION:

FAMILY HISTORY:

SOCIAL BACKGROUND:

RELIGION:

HOBBIES:

POSITIVE CHARACTERISTICS:

NEGATIVE CHARACTERISTICS:

GOALS:

LIKES: DISLIKES:

FRIENDS: ENEMIES:

CHARACTER ARC/DEVELOPMENT:

ADDITIONAL CHARACTER DETAILS FOR:

104

CHARACTER NAME :

NICKNAME/ALIAS:

AGE:

DATE OF BIRTH:

WHERE ARE THEY FROM?:

CURRENT LOCATION:

EDUCATION:

PHYSICAL DESCRIPTION:

FAMILY HISTORY:

SOCIAL BACKGROUND:

RELIGION:

HOBBIES:

POSITIVE CHARACTERISTICS:

NEGATIVE CHARACTERISTICS:

GOALS:

LIKES: DISLIKES:

FRIENDS: ENEMIES:

CHARACTER ARC/DEVELOPMENT:

ADDITIONAL CHARACTER DETAILS FOR:

CHARACTER NAME :

NICKNAME/ALIAS:

AGE:

DATE OF BIRTH:

WHERE ARE THEY FROM?:

CURRENT LOCATION:

EDUCATION:

PHYSICAL DESCRIPTION:

FAMILY HISTORY:

SOCIAL BACKGROUND:

RELIGION:

HOBBIES:

POSITIVE CHARACTERISTICS:

NEGATIVE CHARACTERISTICS:

GOALS:

LIKES: DISLIKES:

FRIENDS: ENEMIES:

CHARACTER ARC/DEVELOPMENT:

CHARACTER NAME :

NICKNAME/ALIAS:

AGE:

DATE OF BIRTH:

WHERE ARE THEY FROM?:

CURRENT LOCATION:

EDUCATION:

PHYSICAL DESCRIPTION:

FAMILY HISTORY:

SOCIAL BACKGROUND:

RELIGION:

HOBBIES:

POSITIVE CHARACTERISTICS:

NEGATIVE CHARACTERISTICS:

GOALS:

LIKES: DISLIKES:

FRIENDS: ENEMIES:

CHARACTER ARC/DEVELOPMENT:

ADDITIONAL CHARACTER DETAILS FOR:

CHARACTER NAME :

NICKNAME/ALIAS:

AGE:

DATE OF BIRTH:

WHERE ARE THEY FROM?:

CURRENT LOCATION:

EDUCATION:

PHYSICAL DESCRIPTION:

FAMILY HISTORY:

SOCIAL BACKGROUND:

RELIGION:

HOBBIES:

POSITIVE CHARACTERISTICS:

NEGATIVE CHARACTERISTICS:

GOALS:

LIKES: DISLIKES:

FRIENDS: ENEMIES:

CHARACTER ARC/DEVELOPMENT:

ADDITIONAL CHARACTER DETAILS FOR:

120

CHARACTER NAME :

NICKNAME/ALIAS:

AGE:

DATE OF BIRTH:

WHERE ARE THEY FROM?:

CURRENT LOCATION:

EDUCATION:

PHYSICAL DESCRIPTION:

FAMILY HISTORY:

SOCIAL BACKGROUND:

RELIGION:

HOBBIES:

POSITIVE CHARACTERISTICS:

NEGATIVE CHARACTERISTICS:

GOALS:

LIKES: DISLIKES:

FRIENDS: ENEMIES:

CHARACTER ARC/DEVELOPMENT:

ADDITIONAL CHARACTER DETAILS FOR:

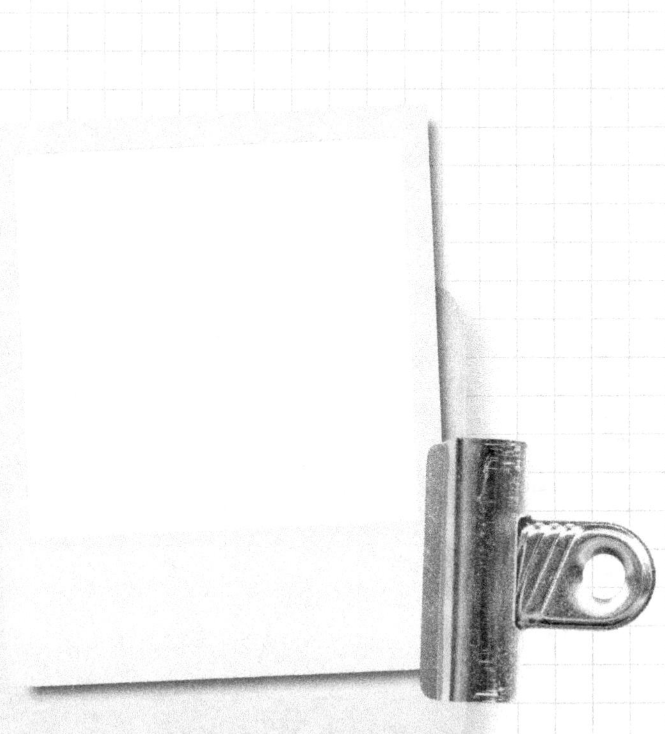

CHARACTER NAME :

NICKNAME/ALIAS:

AGE:

DATE OF BIRTH:

WHERE ARE THEY FROM?:

CURRENT LOCATION:

EDUCATION:

PHYSICAL DESCRIPTION:

FAMILY HISTORY:

SOCIAL BACKGROUND:

RELIGION:

HOBBIES:

POSITIVE CHARACTERISTICS:

NEGATIVE CHARACTERISTICS:

GOALS:

LIKES: DISLIKES:

FRIENDS: ENEMIES:

CHARACTER ARC/DEVELOPMENT:

ADDITIONAL CHARACTER DETAILS FOR:

CHARACTER NAME :

NICKNAME/ALIAS:

AGE:

DATE OF BIRTH:

WHERE ARE THEY FROM?:

CURRENT LOCATION:

EDUCATION:

PHYSICAL DESCRIPTION:

FAMILY HISTORY:

SOCIAL BACKGROUND:

RELIGION:

HOBBIES:

POSITIVE CHARACTERISTICS:

NEGATIVE CHARACTERISTICS:

GOALS:

LIKES: DISLIKES:

FRIENDS: ENEMIES:

CHARACTER ARC/DEVELOPMENT:

CHARACTER NAME :

NICKNAME/ALIAS:

AGE:

DATE OF BIRTH:

WHERE ARE THEY FROM?:

CURRENT LOCATION:

EDUCATION:

PHYSICAL DESCRIPTION:

FAMILY HISTORY:

SOCIAL BACKGROUND:

RELIGION:

HOBBIES:

POSITIVE CHARACTERISTICS:

NEGATIVE CHARACTERISTICS:

GOALS:

LIKES: DISLIKES:

FRIENDS: ENEMIES:

CHARACTER ARC/DEVELOPMENT:

ADDITIONAL CHARACTER DETAILS FOR:

CHARACTER NAME :

NICKNAME/ALIAS:

AGE:

DATE OF BIRTH:

WHERE ARE THEY FROM?:

CURRENT LOCATION:

EDUCATION:

PHYSICAL DESCRIPTION:

FAMILY HISTORY:

SOCIAL BACKGROUND:

RELIGION:

HOBBIES:

POSITIVE CHARACTERISTICS:

NEGATIVE CHARACTERISTICS:

GOALS:

LIKES: DISLIKES:

FRIENDS: ENEMIES:

CHARACTER ARC/DEVELOPMENT:

CHARACTER NAME :

NICKNAME/ALIAS:

AGE:

DATE OF BIRTH:

WHERE ARE THEY FROM?:

CURRENT LOCATION:

EDUCATION:

PHYSICAL DESCRIPTION:

FAMILY HISTORY:

SOCIAL BACKGROUND:

RELIGION:

HOBBIES:

POSITIVE CHARACTERISTICS:

NEGATIVE CHARACTERISTICS:

GOALS:

LIKES: DISLIKES:

FRIENDS: ENEMIES:

CHARACTER ARC/DEVELOPMENT:

ADDITIONAL CHARACTER DETAILS FOR:

CHARACTER NAME :

NICKNAME/ALIAS:

AGE:

DATE OF BIRTH:

WHERE ARE THEY FROM?:

CURRENT LOCATION:

EDUCATION:

PHYSICAL DESCRIPTION:

FAMILY HISTORY:

SOCIAL BACKGROUND:

RELIGION:

HOBBIES:

POSITIVE CHARACTERISTICS:

NEGATIVE CHARACTERISTICS:

GOALS:

LIKES: DISLIKES:

FRIENDS: ENEMIES:

CHARACTER ARC/DEVELOPMENT:

ADDITIONAL CHARACTER DETAILS FOR:

CHARACTER NAME :

NICKNAME/ALIAS:

AGE:

DATE OF BIRTH:

WHERE ARE THEY FROM?:

CURRENT LOCATION:

EDUCATION:

PHYSICAL DESCRIPTION:

FAMILY HISTORY:

SOCIAL BACKGROUND:

RELIGION:

HOBBIES:

POSITIVE CHARACTERISTICS:

NEGATIVE CHARACTERISTICS:

GOALS:

LIKES: DISLIKES:

FRIENDS: ENEMIES:

CHARACTER ARC/DEVELOPMENT:

ADDITIONAL CHARACTER DETAILS FOR:

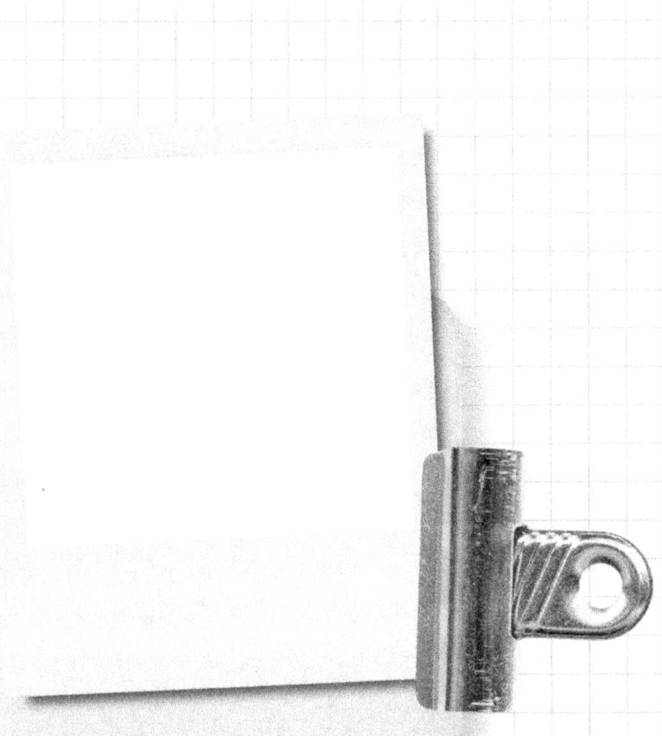

CHARACTER NAME :

NICKNAME/ALIAS:

AGE:

DATE OF BIRTH:

WHERE ARE THEY FROM?:

CURRENT LOCATION:

EDUCATION:

PHYSICAL DESCRIPTION:

FAMILY HISTORY:

SOCIAL BACKGROUND:

RELIGION:

HOBBIES:

POSITIVE CHARACTERISTICS:

NEGATIVE CHARACTERISTICS:

GOALS:

LIKES: DISLIKES:

FRIENDS: ENEMIES:

CHARACTER ARC/DEVELOPMENT:

CHARACTER NAME :

NICKNAME/ALIAS:

AGE:

DATE OF BIRTH:

WHERE ARE THEY FROM?:

CURRENT LOCATION:

EDUCATION:

PHYSICAL DESCRIPTION:

FAMILY HISTORY:

SOCIAL BACKGROUND:

RELIGION:

HOBBIES:

POSITIVE CHARACTERISTICS:

NEGATIVE CHARACTERISTICS:

GOALS:

LIKES: DISLIKES:

FRIENDS: ENEMIES:

CHARACTER ARC/DEVELOPMENT:

ADDITIONAL CHARACTER DETAILS FOR:

CHARACTER NAME :

NICKNAME/ALIAS:

AGE:

DATE OF BIRTH:

WHERE ARE THEY FROM?:

CURRENT LOCATION:

EDUCATION:

PHYSICAL DESCRIPTION:

FAMILY HISTORY:

SOCIAL BACKGROUND:

RELIGION:

HOBBIES:

POSITIVE CHARACTERISTICS:

NEGATIVE CHARACTERISTICS:

GOALS:

LIKES: DISLIKES:

FRIENDS: ENEMIES:

CHARACTER ARC/DEVELOPMENT:

ADDITIONAL CHARACTER DETAILS FOR:

CHARACTER NAME :

NICKNAME/ALIAS:

AGE:

DATE OF BIRTH:

WHERE ARE THEY FROM?:

CURRENT LOCATION:

EDUCATION:

PHYSICAL DESCRIPTION:

FAMILY HISTORY:

SOCIAL BACKGROUND:

RELIGION:

HOBBIES:

POSITIVE CHARACTERISTICS:

NEGATIVE CHARACTERISTICS:

GOALS:

LIKES: DISLIKES:

FRIENDS: ENEMIES:

CHARACTER ARC/DEVELOPMENT:

CHARACTER NAME :

NICKNAME/ALIAS:

AGE:

DATE OF BIRTH:

WHERE ARE THEY FROM?:

CURRENT LOCATION:

EDUCATION:

PHYSICAL DESCRIPTION:

FAMILY HISTORY:

SOCIAL BACKGROUND:

RELIGION:

HOBBIES:

POSITIVE CHARACTERISTICS:

NEGATIVE CHARACTERISTICS:

GOALS:

LIKES: DISLIKES:

FRIENDS: ENEMIES:

CHARACTER ARC/DEVELOPMENT:

ADDITIONAL CHARACTER DETAILS FOR:

CHARACTER NAME :

NICKNAME/ALIAS:

AGE:

DATE OF BIRTH:

WHERE ARE THEY FROM?:

CURRENT LOCATION:

EDUCATION:

PHYSICAL DESCRIPTION:

FAMILY HISTORY:

SOCIAL BACKGROUND:

RELIGION:

HOBBIES:

POSITIVE CHARACTERISTICS:

NEGATIVE CHARACTERISTICS:

GOALS:

LIKES: DISLIKES:

FRIENDS: ENEMIES:

CHARACTER ARC/DEVELOPMENT:

ADDITIONAL CHARACTER DETAILS FOR:

CHARACTER NAME :

NICKNAME/ALIAS:

AGE:

DATE OF BIRTH:

WHERE ARE THEY FROM?:

CURRENT LOCATION:

EDUCATION:

PHYSICAL DESCRIPTION:

FAMILY HISTORY:

SOCIAL BACKGROUND:

RELIGION:

HOBBIES:

POSITIVE CHARACTERISTICS:

NEGATIVE CHARACTERISTICS:

GOALS:

LIKES: DISLIKES:

FRIENDS: ENEMIES:

CHARACTER ARC/DEVELOPMENT:

CHARACTER NAME :

NICKNAME/ALIAS:

AGE:

DATE OF BIRTH:

WHERE ARE THEY FROM?:

CURRENT LOCATION:

EDUCATION:

PHYSICAL DESCRIPTION:

FAMILY HISTORY:

SOCIAL BACKGROUND:

RELIGION:

HOBBIES:

POSITIVE CHARACTERISTICS:

NEGATIVE CHARACTERISTICS:

GOALS:

LIKES: DISLIKES:

FRIENDS: ENEMIES:

DEVELOPMENT:

ADDITIONAL CHARACTER DETAILS FOR:

CHARACTER NAME :

NICKNAME/ALIAS:

AGE:

DATE OF BIRTH:

WHERE ARE THEY FROM?:

CURRENT LOCATION:

EDUCATION:

PHYSICAL DESCRIPTION:

FAMILY HISTORY:

SOCIAL BACKGROUND:

RELIGION:

HOBBIES:

POSITIVE CHARACTERISTICS:

NEGATIVE CHARACTERISTICS:

GOALS:

LIKES: DISLIKES:

FRIENDS: ENEMIES

CHARACTER ARC/DEVELOPMENT:

ADDITIONAL CHARACTER DETAILS FOR:

9 781691 546145